"[Sullivan] is a poet of steel shavings, of semidetached feeling, of unexpected links and impieties and unpropitious implications. She's writing criticism of daily life—criticism of the state of her own soul."   —Dwight Garner, *The New York Times Book Review*

"Sullivan's voice has a suppleness that canters within the formal constraints she imposes on it . . . She's an exquisite image-maker and analogist."   —Declan Ryan, *The New York Review of Books*

"Majestic . . . [Hannah Sullivan's] authority, reach and ambition are exhilarating. Her metaphorical scope is that of the internet."
     —Lavinia Greenlaw, *London Review of Books*

"Hannah Sullivan's language thrills at the cellular level . . . Sullivan has made Wordsworth's rhetorical 'Was it for this [. . .]' bruisingly existential."   —Sylee Gore, *Poetry Foundation*

"Rare, sympathetic, exceptionally readable . . . Sullivan moves instinctively between forms as if stepping from one room into another, which is fitting because her subject is, in part, places she has called home . . . Sullivan's wonderful, satisfyingly condensed writing counters precariousness and sees off futility."
     —Kate Kellaway, *The Observer* (London)

"Sullivan's *Three Poems* was . . . the kind of book people lowered their voices to speak about, recommending it to friends like a well-guarded family recipe . . . *Was It for This* is continuous, in many ways, with *Three Poems* . . . Tragedy is never cheapened or sensationalized, and in her attention to the disgraceful facts of the [Grenfell Tower] fire, Sullivan achieves something often attempted but rarely pulled off: a political poetry that goes beyond

the individual. Her poetry shows the political and personal are inseparable." —Andrew Koenig, *The Harvard Review*

"Sullivan's way of proceeding, her own net of sound and syntax, feels equally suited to pastoral as to urban scenes . . . Sullivan—who is also a Henry James scholar—arranges for the river of her single book, or of her three long poems, to flow around and through public history." —Stephanie Burt, *The Yale Review*

"[Sullivan] artfully explores space, time, and loss, planting us concretely in settings from her childhood and adulthood while exploring the abstracts of aging. She attempts to define what makes time, time, eventually yielding to its nothingness, its inherent ungraspable qualities . . . Sullivan's perspective is warm and flawlessly recounted, yet the despair comes through from a forty-something woman who has lived, has regrets, and wants more time." —Meredith Boe, *Chicago Review of Books*

"*Was It for This* is transcendent . . . Structure, plot, themes, tone, and diction all combine to consecrate the ordinary alongside the exceptional." —Leigh Rastivo, *The Arts Fuse*

"Elegant, affecting, and verbally memorable . . . Sullivan is quite brilliant at the level of the individual phrase, the strangely turned observation." —Brian Dillon, *4Columns*

Teresa Walton

HANNAH SULLIVAN

Was It for This

Hannah Sullivan lives in London and teaches English at Oxford. She studied classics at Cambridge and then lived in the United States for a decade. *Three Poems*, her debut collection, was awarded the 2018 T. S. Eliot Prize and the John Pollard Foundation International Poetry Prize.

ALSO BY HANNAH SULLIVAN

Three Poems

WAS IT FOR THIS

WAS IT FOR THIS

Hannah Sullivan

FARRAR, STRAUS AND GIROUX

NEW YORK

Farrar, Straus and Giroux
120 Broadway, New York 10271

Originally published in 2023 by Faber & Faber Ltd, Great Britain
Published in the United States in 2023 by Farrar, Straus and Giroux
First American paperback edition, 2024

Library of Congress Control Number: 2022949013
Paperback ISBN: 978-0-374-61286-3

Our books may be purchased in bulk for promotional, educational,
or business use. Please contact your local bookseller or the Macmillan
Corporate and Premium Sales Department at 1-800-221-7945, extension 5442,
or by email at MacmillanSpecialMarkets@macmillan.com.

www.fsgbooks.com
Follow us on social media at @fsgbooks

P1

for my mother

Contents

TENANTS   1

WAS IT FOR THIS   21

HAPPY BIRTHDAY   75

Acknowledgements   105

TENANTS

                                        . . . but as
Fishes glide, leaving no print where they pass,
Nor making sound . . .

14 June 2017
00:54 BST

   1.

To think of an event, a thing that happened,
To understand how vague it was,
How confused, uneventful, out of time.

To see the silver pencil in the sky
And hear the whistle of a V2 bomb.
Old women running out with not much on,
It was the last year of the war and they were tired.

To touch their wagging plaits of fine grey hair
And watch the renovation of the tower,
Built in the emptiness the bombs had cleared,
Where blouses flagged along the washing line.

   *

John Lewis was being built. Cranes snapped
Like nutcrackers on little nubs of sky
Or slowly dipped their jibs in courteous lines.
The markets faltered, penthouses were passed
Between the agencies, and even when the monies
Were exchanged remained unoccupied,
The views they might afford unseen, unshown.
Work stopped on digging double basements out,
Especially in the streets that ran due north.
Some of the laminated fakebrick walls blew down,

Exposing missing house parts, cellars gone,
The chunky yellow lumps of London clay
Which, after being machine-regurgitated,
Looked like scone dough, fine crumbs of butter-flour.

*

We watched a video of a beehive being cleaned out in spring.
Somewhere in Arkansas a man was hacking jaggedly,
Scraping with a blunt and shiny metal tool,
Ripping at rotten comb, the cells perforated, sunken,
Ropey with the shaggy clumped detritus of the bees,
Pitiful he said, tugging soft handfuls of it loose.
It looked like that grey stuff inside the hoover,
Or rockwool in the attic that you emptied with your mother,
The house being sold.

*

On dry grey days we went to Holland Park.
The little children's playground was revamped.
It cost a million pounds and looked the same.
I sat down on a bench, beside my pram,
Ignoring any email that came in,
Unravelling a racetrack from a Chelsea bun,
The baby on my lap, for safety sniffing him,
Addicted to his warm, sweet yeasty smell,
The buttered popcorn of the breastmilk nappies.
I was absconding from the life that I had had,
Committed to being small, nutlike, enshelled.
My phone was turned to silent so the calls just flashed.
I threw some sozzled raisins to the birds.

Some of the pigeons slept, their heads tucked in,
Little steelwool scourers for the sink.

The others gulped at crumbs beside the bins,
As a child made blowball from a stale baguette.
Some picked the breast meat off a fallen crow,
The cavity they left was smooth and clean,
Like something you could use to scoop ice cream.

*

The baby cinema was mostly empty, the coffee counter closed,
The custom of free bourbon biscuits was disused.

The few remaining babies were less lusty, cowed,
And because the room was still, sound ricocheted around

As the stooped experimental ghost, sheeted in white,
With large, skewed bloodhound holes cut out across the eyes

Grabbed bowls and plates out of the dated dark pine cupboards
And hurled them at the wall, watching his family eat their supper.

A whirling discus thrower, speeding up, until his hands met air.
And then he stood remorsefully, regarding the porcelain
    splinters,

The milk pooling on terracotta and, underneath the table,
The improbably entire half plate his wife picked up and cradled,

Like a piece of terra rubra found at Verulamium,
Pinned to another piece in a small countryside museum.

*

If you can make yourself into a nut, I thought,
Like the one that older boy lobs round the slide,
The peanuts rattling in their woody skin . . .

If you can make yourself into a nut, unshelled,
i.e. cased in your own space and fibrous brown,
Pitted with crevices, lunar reservoirs . . .

If you can make yourself into a nut.
If you can Marie Kondo everything.
Fold vertically, give things away.
Be less.

2.

Meanwhile, the smell of acetone in public places
And terror in the eyes of a police horse,
The rider lying thrown. Leaflets explained:
These are normal operations designed
To sabotage hostile reconnaissance.
We may use sniffer dogs or arms,
The operation could last for any length of time,
Involving various asset types and numbers.
The aim is principally counter-terrorist.
If you see officers patrolling @LondonTransport
Remember #TogetherWeveGotItCovered.

*

My days contracted to a mile by pram.
Most mornings I spent in the pharmacy
Or nursing in the French patisserie,
Now boarded up and in receivership,
Where the spy found naked in a North Face holdall
Was known to sit and drink Americano,
Meet visitors. Maybe a Russian couple.
Numerous reconstructions were attempted
By experts in confinement and contortionists.
The bag was found inside a bathtub, locked.
A parachutist tried 300 times but couldn't fit,
The second expert got inside but couldn't pull the zip.
A self-shot video showed the decomposing man

Swaying from behind in high-heeled boots,
Brushing the dust from cherry patent leather.

I watched the other mothers at the counter.
They waited, one arm rocking a closed pram,
Or dancing slowly on stiff hips, cupping a warm
Full nappy in a sling. They say it isn't tar
That black stuff she's still bringing up.
Who knows. The surgery is always closed,
Or else you stand with the speaker function on,
Picking the Rorschach blots of limestone off your tea,
Passed between a frizzled Lennon song
And you're seventh in the queue, please hold.

The pharmacist was always slurping something,
His mugs said Daddy or Keep Calm and Carry On.
I asked him what was safe to use on eczema,
He said E45 and rang a huge tub up.
But what would happen in the case of fire, I asked,
Making my hands flat, flammable, the residues on clothes.

*

During the past MONTH have the following concerned you:
Flying, seeing blood, injections, heights, being locked in, dying?

If so, it may be helpful to give details in the box below.
I wrote down Soviet-era nerve agents, nail bombs, the fire.

Then I watched his gaze move past me to the pavement,
A man was wheeling lemons, greenish, knobbly, down a ramp.

He piled the boxes badly on the pallet truck, some open,
A lemon rolled between two yellow lines.

My homework for next time was writing out my birth story,
For many of his clients it was a turning point in therapy.

Because what happened in the world is never absolute,
Because it wasn't me myself, because no story is the truth,

He would encourage me to visualise it on TV.
I might be sitting on a sheepskin rug drinking a rooibos tea,

Reading a magazine, painting my nails Chanel Le Vernis.
The point was to be watching from a space outside my body,

Not even looking at the documentary of my life on screen,
Until I picked up the remote and pressed FF and RW

And watched it whizzing by in random snapshot silhouettes
Bisected by a thin white line that jumped, a glitch effect.

The point was for it all to be unreal, dissociated from me,
Just this thing on VHS I'd seen so many times it bored me.

*

Halfway through a heatwave, soon the solstice.
The milk sweats, dawn at 5, bad sleep again,
That cloistered smell – old water, dying flowers –
Then <ping>, an email from America.
This fire in Kensington, are you OK?

I'd heard the helicopters in the night,
Scooping the baby from the bassinet,
And up again to change my clothes and pad,
Sweat-chilled, the lochia golden now,
The texture of a custard dim-sum bun.

But I'd imagined them on railway lines,
The suicide's ambivalence, a joy-ride,
The suspect slipping in the tangled junction.
To the extent, that is, that I had thought at all,
Cocooned, minutely logging feeds,
Self-made servant of my selfish genes,
A mile away.

Downstairs I watched the fire all morning on TV:
Fine spray of metalworking sparks,
The upper windows blown out clean to holes
And, lower down, the water jets' neat
Ornamental arcs, trained metres short.
People standing on the forecourt with
Only the things they were standing in.
The sulphurous smoke, a thick wedge
Thinning northwards, debris everywhere,
The trees never more magnificent.

At night (because there might be toxic fumes
Because the baby ought to stay at home),
I went by car to drop off baby things:
Pampers size 0, wet wipes, unworn vests.
They said that at this time there was no room.

                *

Now when I walked into that street, walked north
It stood   it was just there.

A blackened shell or husk, the papers said,
A blackened skeleton. A mausoleum.
Our disgrace.
What I saw was still changing daily,

The texture crinkled, corrugated, lacy,
Sometimes close-worked and intricate,
Like the feathery boa round the window-panes,
But also stubbled, coppery, distressed,
Fine hessian hairs on just-ripe blackberries.
And all the widows that you saw in Greece
                                    just sitting
All the mascara shades the drugstore has
From very black to blackest black black pearl
                            new death is onyx.
Hands in their laps a line of women sitting
Outside the kafeneion by the port.
There, by the stone slab with the fishheads on.

3.

Dogs throw themselves against the fence,
The slip road turning grey,
And by the windows residents
Still kneel at dawn to pray,

Or look out with their backpacks on
Towards the nodding cranes
The tin sheds and the holding stacks
In empty space of planes.

Part of each driver driving on,
Another part stays put,
Effusing over building ground
As fine exhaust and soot.

*

Before the fire, the firemen weren't informed
That rainscreen cladding might be flammable,
Or that the staircase had been breached by drilling,
Which meant that smoke dense with particulate
Leapt choking up the only exit route,
Warping the melted plastic safety lights,
As water sluiced and fell in useless panes
And hoses tangled on the floor and melted,
Prising ajar the fire-resistant doors
That families had plugged with bits of cloth.

In the case of the deceased, we can compare
The point at which the person was recovered
To that person's origin within the tower,
Thereby mapping their movement as a vector.
There was a pattern of upwards migration,
Fifteen residents climbed up to the 23rd floor,
Joining the eleven people already there,
A decision that was invariably fatal,
Some started hanging sheets, some jumped.
I felt the body glancing on my back,
A fireman said, I saw the leg pop off.
It sprang off with its slipper on, it ran.

Firefighting operations were exceptional,
Dynamic risk assessment became requisite:
By 1am, 'Stay Put' should have been obsolete.
But this report is avowedly provisional.
We await further evidentiary material.

                *

Dreams people had: dreams of a dream
Of sleepwalking in air,
Of pickling limes and aubergine
And driving east for Uber,

I went to Westfield to buy oil
To put into her hair
I charged the phone and made a call
I walked into a fire,

I watched him get the hamster out
And put it on her knee,
The sheets of fire were long and white
And fell down as debris.

I saw the father giving up,
The television on,
As Pedro Pony stayed asleep,
And Peppa started crying,

And then he started soaking towels
And pushed her, shoving down
Into the smell like nothing else,
And ran and fell and ran.

Outside they pinned him to the floor,
And someone put a line in.
I dreamed about an open door,
The smell of lamb and cumin.

But in the footage on TV
As the whiteness billowed higher,
I saw someone who looked like me
Just waving at a window.

                *

In the burned-out tower dawn happens in an instant,
Like dye fluorescing through a leaf's venation,
Or the route out of a crowded cinema at night,
A blazing EXIT HERE illumination.

4.

If you can think about the stencilled words
Above the fire-resistant cot he had just built,
Twinkle Twinkle Little Star
Do you know how loved you are?

If you can think about the child whose favourite song
Was *run, run, as fast as you can,*
You can't catch me I'm the gingerbread man,
And see the kitchen as it was, the fridge,
The saffron crumbling in the stewing fish,
And then the rectangle of ash it is . . .

If you can hear the bombs that razed the site,
Old women running out with not much on,
It was the last year of the war and they were tired,
And touch their wagging, greasy braids of hair . . .

You'll see the vacancy it always was,
The eagerness with which all things disperse.

*

When we were children there was never snow, it didn't come,
Or if it came it was a few flakes from the classroom window,
Already losing structure by the time you crossed the room
And set the fine unbroken red-tipped pencil-shaving down.

That was the first year of the snow, the first year in the tower,
The first year he came round, you met him at the ground,
Your fingers brushed his fumbling on the button for the floor,
Then tea in the new mugs, two spoons of demerara sugar.

His fingers traced out something on your hand, a tickly line,
A rising feeling everywhere and then he lay you down,
Your neck was in the beanbag, the blue corduroy was soft,
That sandy sound, his palm finding your waist and hips.

One of your little brother's fireman stickers on the rug,
You peeled it off and balled it up, the sky was looking ill,
The sickly colour of a sponge cake taken out too soon,
A heartbeat getting harder underskin, his skin or yours.

The trains had vanished on the track, your pulses tightening
And narrowing, a feeling of being winched and winching in,
Distance diminished in the sky, the yellowness was gone,
A rush of blood him you a gulp the body swallowing.

And then the snow: to start with pixelated, clean,
Then puffy and distressed like rockwool ceiling insulation,
A lining from the inside or a kind of household cladding,
A whiteness waiting to be written on by brightness.

*

To see the length and breadth and depth of hell.
The water sluicing down the stairs, the hoses reaching out a
     hand, not hoses, soft . . .
The fetus slowing, losing his newly acquired skills,
His fingers no longer bothering to touch his newgrown hair,
His mother carried out, face soot-side up, his mother running
     large with him back up the stairs
Into the smoke the cyanide her mind her hand

Her hand the memory of her daughter's wrist being lost,
Rescuing the already born because.

To meditate on the efficiency of the placenta, its vascularity,
The chunks of liver, the swift diffusion across the intervillous
    spaces.
On children lost, stillborn. The word stillbirth.
The man who planned to tie his daughter to his chest,
Step into air, flip up,
Go lying on his back to break her fall.
And on the way that baby was delivered,
The silence as they dressed him this one time,
His mother's body thumping to the side,
The midwife's fingers fumbling on the poppers.
His mother waking up evacuated, masked.

To hear the short cough petulant the hosepipe made, being
    trodden on,
Staccato of the skull against the stairs, the water jets,
The slop of firemen wrestling the carcass down, the heaving dog,
And outside underneath a tree at dawn
The body laid out on the ground.
That rattling sound.

You'll know it when you hear it
the new cassettes deforming
the polyethylene
Hello
Did you say T for tango?
A four-floor building, fine
I said they're on their way
The fire brigade are coming

I said they're on the way
OK?
You only called just now
Look

I said you need to stay
It's only ten past one

It's still a six-pump fire
The stairs are free of smoke still
You're safest in your flat
Conditions on the stairs
I think there is one yes
Have the fire brigade been yet?
I'm having trouble hearing
It's balancing the risks
You don't know what's outside
You need to get wet towels

Hello

I said it's the *fourth floor*

OK?
Can you be quick look
Please?

I said it's jumping up
Look!
It's going up and over
and it's going down
Hello?
Hello?
And now it's ten to two
It's very dark in here
The stairs are very hot
Is the helicopter there?
It's getting hard to breathe now

It's very dark in here
The windows blowing out
It's very hot in here
It's very hot
Oh please

I'll keep you on the line
They're coming for you now
What floor is it you're on   I'm calling from the Westway
But look it's your decision

                                    You want to send them all, love
I said it's your decision   You want to send them all
I said it's up to you
If you need to leave
Just go
Hello?

                *

And when the judge says, *if we may,*
Just to help me fix the timeline in my mind
You think there was no timeline in my mind,
I don't remember that specific time.
What I remember was the whiteness of the fire
A perfect whiteness, magnetising . . .
And carrying bodies down,
Soft hoses underfoot, one reached its hand
Snagged at my leg, how heavy they all were,
The dead ones lighter than the living, though.
I took nine down and eight survived
I felt the ninth soul leave, it lightened,
I heard it go, a slippery sound, a changing tense.
And then the heat inside the concrete,
Everywhere the fire had been, heat on my spine.
We stood there with the hoses turned right down,
The kitchen had no structure, it was tissue.
We painted it with droplets and, at 5,
I looked out of a hole, and it was summer.
The glass had fallen in a sheet straight down,
New birds now adults sang.

*

To walk into the flat where it all started,
And see the fridge the square it had no depth,
It would have crumbled under water jets.
To walk out of the bridgehead into dawn.

Outside this incandescence neither green
Nor yellow in the gardens, June, the birds.
The traffic on the Westway was still sparse
And stately as the drivers rubbernecked.

To say the caller's name and hold the line,
To keep the caller there until the end.
To walk into the almost-longest day,
The tinnitus of silence after sound.

Outside this incandescence in the gardens,
The sprinklers turning in the garden squares.

WAS IT FOR THIS

                    Was it for this
That one, the fairest of all rivers, loved
To blend his murmurs with my nurse's song . . . ?

1. London, 1980s

Lisle Street, late eighties:
a slowly surging crowd
between bow-fronted houses,
the lanterns jittering,
and the ducks slung onto hooks
their loose skin Coppertone.

I was riding piggyback
watching a papier-mâché
trimmed with velvet lion
tap demurely at a cabbage
with its nose, the cabbage
dangled from a window
and the lion on threads,
its parted mouth a rictus
of Big Bird delight, but deader,
the glassy tacked-on eyes
unmoved by failure or eventually
(more rain, a helping hand) success . . .

And then, the ceremony over,
some sense of purpose wiped,
the faces in their winter hats
turning away, dispersing,
my father dropped his fag
half-smoked, resteadying me,
and it tucked its orange tail
into its tip, protectively.

SUNDAY OUGHT TO BE A DAY OF REST
NWOTANIHC OT EMOCLEW.

Swiss Centre, then the tube.
As the glockenspiel rang 5
the cows and men in breeches
started going round and nodding
up and down, grass-nibbling,
pressing cheese. *Take this*,
Dad said, his hand warm with a coin,
you can put it in his cup.
But then he flinched me back.
Why are his cheeks like that?
I meant the rum and raisin scabs
and dropped the coin which span
off giddily, the tarmac
faceted and bright with rain.

*

The people in sleeping bags outside the station were sleeping rough. But why are they lying down now, I asked. There was still a stripe of light above the rooftops.

On the Tube I watched our faces dissolving in the window opposite and my father talked about his new job at British Telecom. He was working on a project to split the London dialling code, 01, into two. The project was called donutisation because the centre would have one code, 071, and the suburbs, where we lived, would be 081. Why? I didn't understand. It was because they had run out of phone numbers. This way, by splitting the city into two, they could add eight million more.

When the doors opened at Baron's Court it was dark and clear outside. A wet breeze fluffed up the *Standard*s lying on the floor.

Everyone I knew lived in a home. Property prices rose.

I learned to think about homes, houses, as a duality. There was the actual house with the exuberant felt-tip marks on the stair walls and the sofa arms shredded to matchsticks by the cat. This house was always getting worse, the stair carpet nubbly and sandy where moths had laid their eggs, the paint chipping, the roof leaking onto balled-up towels. It needed underpinning. Then there was the house as an asset, mortgaged, pinned mysteriously to other assets, the dollar, the yen, coffee and pork futures. No matter how shabby the real house became, it remained a *good investment*.

There was always some heroism, some sacrifice, in the way that our parents had acquired the house; someone had fallen out of the chain, been gazumped; they'd had to eat beans for six months saving for the deposit; for years they only had space heaters. And as soon as the house was acquired it became an impossible purchase. We were lucky. We had stretched ourselves. The iron curtain, which I imagined as a stiff, but ultimately retractable garage door, was lifting. The Berlin Wall was about to come down.

When it did, a girl in my class brought some of the pieces into school and the teacher carefully picked them one by one, like duck eggs, out of the plastic Tesco bag. They were small and disappointing, irregular bits of concrete, some plastered and painted. It looked as if the wall had simply slumped to rubble.

*

My nan lived in Sheffield in a council house on the Southey Green estate. The bathroom was downstairs because my grandfather was ill; he developed emphysema in his forties after working in a steel factory. After he died, she sometimes found it hard to sleep.

I wake up every night, she said, but I don't bother about it now, if it's three or four. I have my book beside the bed and I read for an hour or two, until I start to drift off again. And if I'm not up until 9, I can still go to the shop for the paper, have my tea, get my jobs done. Can't I?

The books were historical novels from the library, hardbacks, vermilion and silver covers, harnessed in those crisp plastic jackets that harbour bits of people's lives. Crumbs, sticky balls of glue or maybe snot, perforated but still conjoined cinema tickets.

When I stayed with her, she used to bring me a plate divided into the four corners of the compass with something separate on each part: little fingers of sandwich with potted beef and brown sauce and a Cox's orange pippin sliced so thin it had already started to darken.

I sat in the beige reclining chair. The soft velveteen cover looked like the dangling ears of a Pound Puppy and it ate up all the light and any spills. Sometimes I was allowed to press the buttons and the footrest shot out, tipping my face to the ceiling. It had been bought for my grandfather when he couldn't breathe. He was 56 when he died. I stayed at home for the funeral and played in the chair. Someone had given me a sherbet lollipop. It took me a long time to excavate all the sherbet with the liquorice stick and I remember the baffling superfluity of pleasure when I realised I was allowed to eat that too.

I still have that feeling sometimes. And that *too*? For *me*?

*

Did he die of emphysema? More *with*, my mother said later, invoking a new rhetoric. It wasn't until last winter – the stuffy, stuck days of the last lockdown – that she told me he had killed himself.

She was the one who wrote off to *Exit* for the leaflets. They said how many pills you needed to take. But then he didn't tell her that he was about to go through with it. Why?

All of this was kept from my grandmother until the appointed day, when he gave her detailed instructions. Both mother and daughter had part of the story, but the two parts didn't make a whole.

It was very important that no one called an ambulance for a full hour. That was what it said in the leaflet. She didn't. She waited the hour out and then she called.

*

My other grandmother lived in Australia. When I was seven, we went to visit her in Perth for five weeks.

Nanny was living with her boyfriend, a term which confused me. Gordon was about the same age as my parents, who were then in their thirties. He had been one of my grandmother's patients in the hospital where, before retiring, she'd worked as a nurse. When we finally arrived, after a journey of many days, Gordon was putting up a large, crinkly white tent, a kind of impromptu extension. We were going to have the motorhome, and they would sleep outside to give us some space.

My bed folded down and I slept right by the corrugated wall, my shoulder under the line of the window. I liked sleeping like this, in the middle of the room, and often pretended to be asleep when I was in fact awake.

*

We went swimming every day, either at the swimming park or in the sea. At the swimming park, I went down the water slides alone. The trickle of water folding and separating around the mat was weirdly mesmerising, and sometimes I sat, and sat, even after the light had changed to green until another child flicked me with the tip of their own mat. Once, my grandmother took me to the jacuzzi and we ate very hot, very salty, fried chicken which fell apart in my hands leaving only the bones. It wasn't clear what to do with the bones and so I put them into the water, surreptitiously, watching the fat fly up and marble the surface. In those years everyone was worried about nuclear war and Australia was the place we might have stayed, if it happened. At the beach, I examined the shapes of the clouds with forensic superstition, trying to pretend to myself that they were mush-room clouds. I was excited by how fast they ticked the sky and moved across it and dissolved again, and sometimes I let myself be carried out just a little too far by the tide, until the clouds and the spluttered water blurred into a confusing spray pattern between me and my parents, oblivious, on the beach.

After a couple of weeks, we rented a car and drove to an aquar-ium to watch dolphins jumping and performing complicated tricks; each trick was accompanied by the threat of an audience-drenching wave. We took a train to an old town, now deserted, where people had panned for gold. It wasn't, my mother said, actually very old. It wasn't even as old as our house. But history was relative. I mustn't be rude. The other worry was the hole in the ozone layer, so I was always slippery with sunscreen. Even so, my skin burned, badly. Some nights I woke with the sunburn stinging and throbbing, on others I lay in bed wicking long strips of dead skin off my shoulders and arms. I enjoyed the moment when a new strip gave way and ran to my will, as I had enjoyed the feeling of the dusty shiny water slipping through my fingers full of small pieces of gold.

*

This was 1988. My grandmother in Sheffield was still in her fifties. She had taken up competitions and whenever we went to visit her (I always crept round the back, to the stable door; I had a special knock) she was reading *Competitor's World* or *Winner's Friend* and writing out slogans in her big, neat looping writing on the back of envelopes.

We ate scones tart with baking powder. Clarty. The man next door had come back from the pub at Christmas and wet the bed. Well, nan said, he'd only left lecky on, hadn't he. Now a new family had moved in, and they kept long-eared rabbits in cages along the fence between the two gardens. The children hardly ever went to school and sometimes they shouted things at nan when she was pegging up the washing. So she wasn't sure if she should buy her house or not. She and my mother talked about it urgently. She had just been given the Right to Buy by Mrs Thatcher. I found this a very impressive phrase, imagining the right being bestowed personally, for good work, like a knighthood.

She exercised the Right and bought it. Twenty-five years later, when she died, she left half of the house to me and half to my mother. Sometimes I look at the photos on Rightmove: the carefully repainted sitting room, the new wallpaper still visible around the chimney breast. But an agent would describe it as ripe for modernising. Ideal for a family looking to put their own stamp on a property.

*

Before, reality had kept withdrawing.
It drew back like a series of low tides
Around an equinoctial new moon.

But now reality was what had been:
The toddler running in his red one-piece
With dinghies on, the matching hat discarded,

The ordinary shell squeezed in his hand,
And in the space around him, which was blue,
The grainy texture of the drizzling sand.

*

When we flew back to London, we moved into a different house. I started at a new school. Somehow, I had failed to realise that this was the purpose of the holiday or, indeed, that it was happening.

In the new kitchen there was an airing cupboard where our cat had six kittens, one born without a tail, but as agile as the others. They hauled themselves up the varnished pine doors and sometimes a small black paw could be seen batting between the slats, the claws slipping out and then retracting. The slats of the airing cupboard doors were varnished, and they were also speckled with perfectly formed drops of shining dark brown. I liked to run my finger over these notches and feel how warm and substantial they were. If you half-closed your eyes, they looked like Marmite.

I didn't remember the New Year's Eve when I'd stayed at home with my nan while my parents went to a party next door, or the ill-timed bang just before midnight. But I did remember the next morning, my father kneeling on the floor, a sharp pine clean smell of sweat, as he cleaned up the debris of his exploded home-brewing equipment.

*

My teacher at the new school was called Mrs Fox. Our interest in her consisted primarily of the desire to know her first name, and sometimes we dialled her number from our parents' phones, furtively. (We found it in the Yellow Pages, under the most probable address.) If she answered, we put the phone down immediately. But, if her husband picked the phone up, we hung on, breathing nervously at a distance. We were holding out for him to say, 'Sheila' or 'Susan' or 'Linda', 'I think it's for you'.

At break time she ate a kiwi fruit with a spoon, as if it were a boiled egg.

When she developed ME, she left our work for a whole month on the board. Among other things, we were meant to write a novel. The other class's teacher sometimes walked in and out of the room to see if we were doing it, which we always were when we heard her soft officious tread. (Those blue court shoes women of my now-age used to wear, with 10-denier navy tights which sagged around the ankle.)

I wrote a story about a boy who lived 'in the middle ages' and wore a 'leather jerkin'. These phrases were tightly packed with a significance I couldn't parse. His hair, I wrote, was 'flaxen' and 'smelled like the Jorvik Viking Museum' (bacon rasher crisps and woodsmoke, it stays with me even now). The other class's teacher wrote 'but HE wouldn't have described it like this, I don't think!' He lived 'before the industrial revolution, when everything was green'.

Before she developed ME, Mrs Fox's son was in the King's Cross fire. She had a very nasty shock, my mother said. Her face was doughy in maths. He had been in and out of hospital but now he was all right, it was only the shock. Someone had probably dropped a cigarette. There were such long escalators, he had been on the escalator and someone had tipped into him and pushed him forwards. Never smoke. *Oh Laura*, the other teacher said, with her sinewy hand with its Celtic rings in the centre of Mrs Fox's back.

*

Our house smelled of washing, which dried in the airing cupboard or over the banisters of the stairs, and animal fat from the roasts. It must also have smelled of cigarettes, because my father smoked inside, but I didn't notice that; maybe nobody did, then.

The idea of a house that I formed was not at all like the house that we lived in. My idea of a house was old metal music stands and framed photos, on white walls, of young parents leaping in the air in their skis. It had no odour; it had no people.

As I grew older, the idea developed: the house was meant to be infinitely large, bright, empty, all uncluttered space and I, the woman, would sit at the centre, at the end of the vanishing lines of perspective, fatless, spare, dressed in black for downtown.

As if the woman were all matter and the space, from which she was rigidly distinct, were anti-matter. So, the entropy being very low, any number of things might happen.

*

During lockdown, as I sat on the bed with my laptop, wasting my two hours of allocated time to work, I read an article about the tiny ad hoc offices that women all over the world were creating to hide from their children.

In St Louis, a computer programmer had tacked a yellow chiffon curtain across a corridor that looked as if it came from a railroad carriage. Her desk was a folding table pushed into the metal fittings of the wall. If she wanted to use the bathroom, she had to text her husband who put *Frozen* on for the children while she crept back into the house and sat asymmetrically on the loo so that the urine hit the shallowest, quietest spot.

In Tel Aviv, a lawyer who lived with three children in a 700-square-foot apartment worked either in her husband's car or in the bathroom, where she squatted on the stool her children used to brush their teeth. Either way, she said equably, every morning she packed her rucksack with nuts and dates, a bottle of water, her laptop, and then said 'goodbye, Mummy's going to work now'.

I cut and pasted the stool into reverse image search and spent a long time looking at pages of Bekväm stools in people's houses, many hacked: covered with a tiny jaunty crocheted cap, a tasselled tam-o'-shanter; distressed; topped with a vase, a map, nubby baskets holding bike helmets.

The article was meant to be about parenting choices. But the way that the camera eye lingered on the casually thrown-together offices, with their touches of whimsy, fairy lights, the Oreo cookies stacked in a tall jar, made me think that it was really about women's eternal yearning for private space.

2.   America, 2000s

Once in turbulence on a 747 to DC, I talked to a woman who was a professional snowboarder. I'd been upgraded. We'd eaten salted hazelnuts and worked through a lump of beef with real serrated metal knives, we had drunk champagne; 9/11 was still a year away. I was too embarrassed to say how afraid I was, so I fixed my face on hers, as if it was forever, and learned so many clearly visualised things about her recent knee injury, her mother in Basingstoke, and the quality of the snow that when I look back at the afternoon it feels (the depth of my absorption) as if I was falling in love. The champagne kept leaving the glass and returning clumsily like someone jumping without bending their knees enough, landing on an upstairs floor. She had those tiny freckles on her cheekbones that only people with cheekbones ever get, as a gloss on their good luck.

At the end of the flight, I wanted to ask her name. Those conversations that accelerate so fast that naming, at first over-familiar, soon becomes inessential and sort of primitive. She must have felt the same way, because in baggage reclaim at Dulles we exchanged details – in the way people did, pen and paper, in 2000.

But my name, very ordinary, felt by then like a betrayal, so instead of Hannah I wrote, for some reason, *Anna*.

Then I took another flight to Boston.

My parents had moved, a few weeks earlier, to another part of the country and so I had more baggage than was sensible for a nine-month stay.

*

Who it was that arrived in the late afternoon and ate a plum, I hardly know.

It was very hot and compressed in Cambridge, and even hotter air shot in bars out of air conditioning units on the street. I unpacked, and then I went to the coffee house over the street and drank an iced coffee because people on American TV were always drinking and toting about iced coffees. I laced it with syrup and cream because that seemed the thing to do and used my plastic straw to fold the ribbons of white and shine into the coffee until it was a flat dun.

In the evening, my landlord's daughter, 13 or 14, took me to the Star Market to get some shopping. She showed me the bananas and then we bought some cereal. I'm not sure if you have bananas in England, she said.

The daylight slid suddenly away as I was unpacking, and the hot night air was full of insects. I went to a deli and sat alone, drinking Sam Adams in a frosted glass, watching the diving Olympics.

Then classes started, the weather turned, huge boy-men appeared everywhere peering out of their fringes, and people invited me to Indian lunch buffets. I enrolled in a course on Weimar intellectual history and said nothing, week after week, as the others discussed Theodor Adorno and Ernst Bloch. But the translated phrases preyed on my imagination: 'the future is the sign outside the No Future night club'; 'the splinter in your eye is the best magnifying glass'. For a poetry workshop I picked up handfuls of maple leaves, large and loose, entire on the road, and wrote haikus as instructed. In the workshop, the professor was kind to me. One of my poems rhymed 'bite' and 'Merlot' and she said it was a good rhyme.

Then the weather turned again and all I seemed to do was trudge back and forwards in the snow with my basket of clothes to the laundromat. Sometimes I slept very late because of the cold, twelve or thirteen hours, and woke confused about which room or house the bed was in. To convince myself to get up I had to rush from the bed and turn the shower to run – wasting the hot water in a show of steam – just to make the room tolerably warm. Sometimes I woke in the middle of the night and heard the landlord shouting upstairs and his wife's voice change, the always-shock of physical pain.

That noise a balloon makes let go.

*

Winter in Boston lasted a long time. All March, boulders of snow and grit had lain around in the streets, melting and refreezing. Eventually they looked like the Brancusi torsos in the art museum, only greyer.

In the first week of April there was a final flurry of snow and then things turned, overnight. On the first warm weekend of the year, I went on a date with the man who owned the coffee house. Possibly he invited me from guilt. One morning when a song came on – something I half knew, I can't even remember what – I asked what it was, and his lip twitched, as if he was trying to muster self-control over tears.

It turned out that the people in the coffee house – certainly all of the people who worked there, and more than one fellow patron – thought that I was deaf. From childhood I had had a mild speech impediment. I just hadn't realised how bad it was, when combined with an unexpected accent. He said defensively, 'Everyone assumed you were lip-reading. Once you said you weren't Australian.'

It was our only date. Classes were about to end, and I wanted to move to New York which represented to me, at 21, in the year 2000, every good thing in the world.

When I asked the landlord if I could sublet the flat for the summer – standing on his landing, at the top of the stairs – he lifted his hand up and I flinched, and, as I flinched, his *no* turned into a growly *yes*.

*

One of the things that New York represented was the possibility of never being in.

The shoddier and more unsatisfactory my accommodation there was – and it was always tiny, shared, filthy and encroached on (the flooding upstairs loo, the dripping air conditioner that I worried would fall to the street, the smell of frying tofu from the Sacred Chow) – the lighter I became. As I sat in my room or apartment in June or on a winter's evening, it made no differ-ence, I felt as if I had nested on top of the street and was, from my perch, now swoopingly part of life itself. From the futon or the beanbag, where I sat pushing at the laptop keys, half of my mind was always elsewhere, waiting for the 11 p.m. text message suggesting a drink, or the whistle underneath the window, or just the slow sound of the street-cleaning machine.

Sunt etiam alii, the school motto: now instantiated. All the walls were thin. Underneath my sublet bed there was a box of practically prehistoric mains-powered sex toys, belonging to another woman. My boyfriend and I touched them carefully. It rained. I came. It rained again, it was dawn, and I went and ran through the Meatpacking District and came back and lay on the bed reading novels about New York until the bar opened.

When the upstairs loo leaked, I had a histrionic conversation with the man who lived in 13G – more for show, televisually, than from conviction – and then I went back into the sublet flat and cleaned up the brown water running all over the floor and thought nothing more of it.

*

Sometimes I will always be in a midtown apartment, nearly dawn, end of summer, the blue nights done, handling a cock that never quite hardens, like a pastry chef whose hands are too warm.

Sometimes I will always be riding the escalator into the Hudson hotel, circa March 2000, realising only in the mirror at the very top all of the ways in which the items attached to my body – including my teeth and vicious eyeliner – are wrong.

Sometimes the fruit shop will always be opening, the wet cellophane retracted from the peaches, which, unripe yesterday, now have a give.

*

All ambitions renounced, the times of day vague, almost always out, I was happy. I talked for hours to people I met in the park or on the street because all the things that people said were interesting to me. I lifted weights. I ate plates of beans and rice, comforted an elderly neighbour who had started to see signs, all over the city, meant only for her, and sheltered from the rain in Barnes and Noble, eking out an iced tea until the paper straw broke down into porridge.

So the days and nights passed, summer following summer, one sublet and then another. We saw David Bowie walking past the Belgian beer bar on West 4th Street. He came past again and smiled, a short conspiratorial smile. When it closed someone usually invited us back, or we invited other people, and stayed up doing what, doing nothing, drinking from red plastic cups until all the ice had gone. Dawn again. The brittleness of jet lag, after a red eye, inconsistent and then urgent. I bought bananas at the corner store, ate Kashi.

A friend had a baby and I watched the baby's mouth snapping on her nipple week after week until, one day, it was pearly with teeth.

On wet summer evenings in August my sense of deferral and rehearsal – there always being another night before the curtain went up – began to turn from lassitude to panic. What if the curtain had been up all along?

I was living with my boyfriend but neither of us had a plan for the following year. My parents were retiring. On the phone, my grandmother could no longer understand what I was saying.

*

The last weekend of the last summer, we ate brunch at the counter of a restaurant on Bleecker with a TV. We were watching Federer v. Nadal at Wimbledon and drinking bottomless Mimosas.

It was because we didn't think it was the last time that we ate brunch in a sports bar on Bleecker Street. At the beginning of the summer, I wore a sprigged muslin dress for Sunday brunch and we consulted Zagat. All of this was so long ago that I bought the long, thin maroon book and stuffed it sideways in my bag until the pages rifled and warped.

All the same, at some point in the fourth set, which Federer lost, 2–6, I had an evil intimation. Everything frozen and shot dissolved, a woman kicked her red shoe against my metal stool, the traffic piled up oppressively outside, and I was suddenly crying over my ketchup-bloodied egg curds. Once the match was over, we went on a day trip to Princeton, to visit an old friend for lunch, but I sniffled all the way around the campus and through an ornamental garden. At some point my watch stopped and I kept, monotonously, asking what time it was, but my boyfriend didn't hear and so we walked on, on, on.

We just managed to make the last train back and I was on the verge of tears all the way, on the subway, past the basketball court, through the brown building corridors. The following morning the mood dissolved, and I went back to being young. But now I had seen the other side and I knew it was all effort and show.

I bought a small leopardskin bag. I went to the Berg and read T. S. Eliot's letters to Virginia Woolf in an attempt to retrieve the summer's purpose. Sangria, rain, ice clinking in the jug to nothing.

The scuffle of the basketball finally finding the hoop.

*

Recurrent nightmares about clocks, misset,
and glass revolving doors in hotel lobbies:
you bounce from one pane where a hand
is pressed so hard it yellows bloodlessly
and smack into the other, oscillating
ché la diritta via era smarrita
between two things that are the same, but faster.

*

The following summer, we moved to San Francisco. It was a list-
less place. By dinner-time, the rest of the western world was in
bed and BBC News page remained almost fixed, without new
news, until morning. No one called or emailed in the evenings,
ever. And everything lacked density, felt thin, crowdless, sort of
occasional: the lantern of the one restaurant in miles leering out
of the fog, at the end of the Muni line; the quiet suburban street
suddenly vanishing in the late afternoon. As a driver, I learned
to crest the top of hills at a smooth even speed, trusting that the
apparently truncated road would continue, sloping gently down-
wards, on the other side of the STOP sign.

The morning after we arrived, a realtor drove us around to view
rental apartments. He kept insisting that this apartment or that
one had very good weather, the micro-climates being so particu-
lar that fog and sun followed completely different scripts from
one street to the next.

The first apartment we saw had sash windows and cornicing.
It was confusingly reminiscent of all the other 'Victorians' that
I'd lived in, including my undergraduate room and our apart-
ment in a red-brick building in Harvard Square. But the deck at
the back looked directly at a massive, still-smouldering heap of
burnt-out timber. The fact that the neighbourhood was gentrify-

ing so fast that landlords were prepared to burn down their own buildings seemed, in his mind, to be a selling point. Developers would create huge value in the Mission. But, of course, I would be a tenant too and didn't want to be incinerated in my bed.

*

Sometimes on the way to work I stopped at a Starbucks in Menlo Park, where I befriended a woman who owned a full-size black poodle puppy. It didn't look at all like a miniature poodle and something about that, and its fast rate of growth, interested me enormously. The poodle wore a range of stripy neckerchiefs. I seem, as far as my photo library goes, to have taken more photos of this poodle, often on my own lap, than any other person or thing in San Francisco.

I was 31. In the nicest non-ironic way, it *literally* never occurred to me to have a baby during these years.

At Starbucks and, even more particularly, in the adjacent pharmacy and the Polish bakery, there was a complete, sagged sense of time's endlessness. The angles of the buildings were odd, and the lighting was too low or too high, and it was never clear how long I was meant to be staying there or what I was doing.

The always wet key on a piece of wood to use the bathroom.

The tanned and speckled but not obviously ancient man in the pharmacy who gave his date of birth, in 2009, as June 1905.

*

I tried to force myself to stay at home and work, but the walls closed around me. I was always restless, inventing errands. To justify my behaviour to myself, I watched a YouTube video, speeded up, of a man in a Manhattan office who was trapped in the elevator for an entire weekend.

The way he moved between the four corners was, at the level of each movement, random, but after a while the general pattern of movement started to seem fatally, pointlessly repetitive. He fianchettoed himself to the corner, launched himself at the opposite side, beat a retreat, and so on. Then he looked through what seemed to be a series of small cards. Heartbreakingly, he occasionally managed to open the door, but was somehow unable to squeeze through it. After 22 hours he slept. And then the same pattern of movement began again. After 40, he pushed the button one more time, the action no different from the previous failed attempts, and the door suddenly opened. He walked out casually as if nothing had happened. Then two engineers came in and fiddled with the buttons, before putting up an 'out of order' sign in the entrance.

Someone had commented on the video: 'that is one of my worst fears right there. i would have killed myself within the hour.' But how would you kill yourself in a lift? My fears revolved around the complete lack of apparatus.

*

After a year – a year of frugal living and opening unwanted store credit cards – we bought a house. What we bought was not really the house, so much as the risk of the house. Our relationship to the building was nervously speculative: my husband's employer provided most of the down-payment and the mortgage company took care of the rest. We got the keys a week before our wedding and had nothing to furnish it with.

It was a beautiful, shabby house with dappled fawn-coloured light fittings and bad feng shui, the front door opening onto the intersection of two roads, both plunging steeply downhill. It had been built in 1906, like many of the other houses we viewed.

Despite not having a sofa, we took out very expensive earthquake insurance.

*

The couple who now lived next door, in the middle apartment, had owned our house in the 1970s and 1980s. They sold it when the last of their three children moved to New York. They were both tall and had sharp handsome faces; they were Catholics from Maryland. They came to San Francisco in the summer of '68, but not for any of the obvious reasons. Mary had been pregnant.

They sometimes had us over to dinner and reminisced about the city's past. Francis cooked and he always served broiled wild salmon, very dry in the mouth. Before he served it – I helped to carry the plates through – he wiped off the white fat with a piece of kitchen paper. It annoyed me that, despite cooking the same meal so frequently, perhaps daily, he hadn't found a way to stop the fish from exuding these curdled bits. The whole thing looked like psoriasis. Later, when I started cooking myself, I had the same problem. I read an article that said, don't feel bad, it happens to everyone, it's just albumin.

Dessert would be some sort of dark berry that stained the table-cloth, rich in anthocyanins, which Mary would eventually smear into the white tablecloth or chew loudly until the juice lipsticked the skin around her mouth. We might take a bottle of heart-healthy pinot noir. There was an element of trade: we were to provide company and interest for Mary, to stimulate her; in turn, when something went wrong with our house, we could knock and ask Francis for help. He seemed to have done a lot of the wiring himself.

*

When I found Mary standing at the edge of Dolores Park sifting the air with her hands, I thought I should probably try to take her home. So, hooking my arm into hers, I tried to guide her – she was stiff, like a toddler, and frightened, like a toddler, but finally assenting – onto the Muni. Then we walked very slowly up 24th Street. 'But this isn't it', she kept saying. 'My road is the valley'. Her face showed no recognition of either house or, when he came down the stairs, her husband who put his arms out to take her.

3. London, 2010s

After two years, we found tenants and rented out the house. We were moving back to London. After another two, we sold it. The offer came during my father's funeral.

My husband was in Wilko buying ten black umbrellas. It was only the end of August, but it was raining with a kind of battered slashing fury. I was wearing, for the very first time, a maternity dress, all of my black skirts and trousers having proved impossible to fasten. I was crying because the leaves being ripped from the trees were the last leaves my father had ever seen, and because I had accidentally deleted the voicemail he'd left me, asking me to buy a paper and a Calippo, three weeks earlier. The book was balanced on the square beginnings of a bump.

Then the email came. We accepted the offer immediately and there was a part of me that was glad to be so completely divested, denuded, shot.

*

The general theme of the day was liquefaction, umbrellas, rain running giddily off the highly lacquered surface of the coffin, the soggy soil, the disappearing spikes of heels. The verges in the graveyard were thin on grass and looked like a teeing ground.

I'd said that I would read a passage from *Four Quartets*. During the service, I'd already started to doubt the passage's relevance, in my father's case, its general tenderness, and even its meaning. But it was too late, the service rolled on, and soon I was clambering around people's knees with a piece of loo roll wedged up my sleeve. *Sorry. Sorry.*

> We shall not cease from exploration
> And the end of all our exploring

> Etc.

What the piece of loo roll couldn't contend with – it was like trying to stem a flooding washing machine with a tea towel – were the long, gelatinous, apparently unabsorbable shiny threads of snot that started running from my nose. As I carried on trying to read, dry-eyed, my arms flapped in the most ridiculous way in the air. I remember thinking *my fingers look like knitting needles.*

The congregation gave a deep-bellied, uneasy laugh, and the whole thing got worse, so, by the time I reached the end of the reading, my father's death had been upstaged by collective embarrassment. I wiped my maternity dress down, but it was striped for the rest of the day with fine, gleaming snail trails of snot.

*

Sitting side-saddle in the ward,
his shape so overfilled with
water that its form was lost,
feet sphinxlike, the dialysis
a daily failure, crying
when he thinks you've gone downstairs,
to pay the car again,
his skin the colour of a mohair bear.

But there you are
behind the panelled door
examining the pattern of the glass,
the houndstooth check of inlaid wire,
whipping up these bright Purell meringues.

And then the yelp you gave,
even the nurse, when something long
and bright shot from his mouth
a thin red velvet carpet
being unfurled in wind
or the tongue of the paper lion
you squealed at, once,
hoisted higher on his shoulders
one new year.

*

After the burial, I talked to my grandmother who had been, when her son died, on her annual summer visit to England. Already small, she seemed to have shrunk to nothing except a quick, realistic, very blue pair of eyes – and her perfume.

He had always been a very good boy, she said. He was her eldest child, and when he had just turned four, she went into hospital to have her youngest. She left a jug of orange squash, and he was in charge of pouring it out for his two younger sisters. He did this without spilling a drop.

Once she came home from the hospital, the council gave him a free nursery place. On the first day, she said, she took him and picked him up to bring him home. On the second day, she took him and told him to remember the route.

Was it far, I said. Did he get back all right?

He left in the middle of the morning, but only because he didn't like it. No one noticed him go, but he was back for lunch. And, no, it wasn't far, only half a mile: just the other side of Chiswick high road.

*

Then we went back to my parents' house and ate scones. There were three sorts of homemade jam, all made from fruit that my father had picked.

The motorhome that they'd bought after retiring was still outside. They preferred it, they said. You had all you needed, and your freedom too.

*

All autumn, the estate agents again. Once I'd bought a maternity coat, I knew I was easy prey. There are photos on my phone of me in the blue duffel coat, very shiny, my legs swollen like plantains underneath, in flats and houses all over northwest London. All I did all autumn was go into other people's homes and ask my husband to take photos of places where we could put a side return.

*

I didn't blame the agents. In fact, my first job was in an estate agent's; I had an instinctive sympathy.

The main task was answering the phone and taking down the caller's number and message. The notepads that we wrote on had a hole at the top and advertised a local dentist. After a few weeks, I was allowed to help with the copy for the weekly listings in the newspaper. Most of the houses that we sold were semis or terraces on long late Victorian streets, each more or less the same as its neighbours, but the agency made an effort to personalise the adverts. 'Grin and tonic – Here's something to put a smile on your face, a good tonic for those homehunting blues'. Neither of these tasks was time-consuming and I spent many afternoons turning the pages of a novel under the desk, the white fan whirring in the background and the glass shopfront smeary in the sun.

Once, when everyone else was out of the office or off sick, I showed a man round a modern, fifties house a few metres from the office. He had been waiting for twenty minutes and I felt more uncomfortable about sitting opposite him as he jiggled his leg and I read my book furtively, than I did about going to get the keys.

The house smelled terrible, the metal casements looked as if they'd been eroded with acid, and so many weeds had broken through the stones in the patio garden that the squares of concrete looked like crazy-paving. A fly throbbed inside the double glazing of the empty bedroom, which had two sets of bed posts, one stark, one faint, pressed out on the carpet.

It was also very cheap, and he was divorcing, and he bought it. For the next year, I took a proprietorial interest in the house. When a cement mixer and skip appeared outside, the front door was painted, and blinds went up on the lidless windows, it gave me a feeling of calm and restitutive rightness.

A year later, there were two bikes chained up to the narrow fence; a year after that, I saw a woman backing out slowly with a pram.

*

After work, I went with my mother to water Mrs Perry's plants. She was at her summer house in Broadstairs for the whole of July.

Her house in Hanwell smelled of mothballs, the jellied pre-chunked meat we fed the cats from tins, and wood polish. She taught the piano and, lustrous, well-maintained, the mahogany grand piano looked years younger than the tapestry-topped stools and G-plan chairs, their teak veneer pale and dusty, which sat alongside it.

Mrs Perry had never been happy here, my mother explained. This was because her real home, the happy house of her early marriage to Fred, had been placed *under compulsory purchase order*. She pointed it out to me, a large Victorian house on a circular plot opposite St Mellitus church. Now it was an old-people's home.

There was absolutely no reason why the council would want to buy our house, a single semi in a long street of identical houses, but it stuck in my mind as a possibility, a provoked small anxiety.

In fact, this forcibly repurchased, now vanished, house under-pins my own. Mrs Perry had no children and no close relations and, when she died, she left me £15,000 in her will. Fifteen years later, on a hot Thanksgiving, I transferred it bit by bit into dollars – a complex and unsettling process, the wi-fi not fast enough, using a borrowed card reader – to provide the deposit for our first house.

At moments of maximum domestic incapacity and anxiety – the paint on the walls peeling away, the bathtub chipped, the

furniture all dusty and wrong and plastic toys everywhere –
I have sometimes wondered if Mrs Perry also bequeathed me
her inability to make a home for myself. But this is frank ingrati-
tude because, without her, I might not have a house at all.

*

In the houses we viewed I found a forward-looking *opacity* sur-
prising. Whole bathroom cabinets filled with useful, obvious
things, like toothpaste and hydrocortisone cream, whereas mine
– which wasn't even a cupboard, only a mirrored bordello night-
stand in a rented flat in Paddington – was already filled with the
trash of lost illusions. Expired sleeping pills, weed-laced lip balm
smuggled back from California. A salt pipe.

For a long time I kept the positive pregnancy test from my sec-
ond pregnancy, until, one day, half sane, I realised that a dipstick
yellow with two-year old urine should be in the bin. I still have,
in a small ziplock bag, the now calcified and black winched stub
of once-green cord.

*

The most appealing houses were invariably occupied by angry
women who smoked in the kitchen or left the unchanged litter
tray out, determined to obstruct and delay the sale for as long as
possible.

Sometimes, some part of the errant husband's body would be
visible in a photo on the fridge, as he knelt down on the beach,
say, holding a toddler's hand.

Otherwise, it was as if he had never been. His existence was
reduced entirely to the single, malevolent role of dispossessing

a middle-aged woman from the house that, you could tell, she'd chosen, designed, decorated, and made into her home.

*

It was, of course, not especially possible to buy these houses. In the end, we bought a blank, beige, carefully tended-to house that had been rented out for several years to a German scientist and his wife.

The heating and hot water schedule that they devised, allowing an extra hour in bed on Saturday, and an extra hour and a half on Sunday, still patterns the rhythm of my life. A kind of counter-point, I like to think. A Protestantism.

*

When we moved in, the house was blander and more unasser-tive than anywhere I'd ever lived. And yet, month by month, it accrued hiding places and cubby holes and seemed to get deeper.

To begin with, my son always hid behind the curtains in the sit-ting room. His short pink legs and some small parts of his body were always visible. Only a few months earlier, he'd believed him-self to be hiding if he covered up his eyes. Then he discovered the cupboard under the stairs and the recess between a bedroom door and a cedar wood box. In the kitchen, he muttered and sang and mumbled as he crashed his IKEA saucepans together. So that whole side of the room was his kitchen. The large, useless square landing at the top of the stairs turned out to be the ideal site for building a circular Duplo train track. Usually, a giraffe topped the leaning tower of the front carriage.

And so it went.

Once we had filled all the cupboards past the point of closing, which took two years, I started forcing myself every few months to put things into a heavy-duty black bag and throw them out.

Halfway through, I always started splitting the bag into three: the things to be thrown out, the things to take to the charity shop, the things to put into the loft.

The things to take to the charity shop I left in black bags in the car for months at a time.

The things to be put in the loft went into large plastic boxes that I bought on Amazon or in Wilko. I nested things into them furtively, as if I was setting up little crime scenes.

Sometimes I imagined that I might aestheticise what was really only paralysis – a stuckness in time, a clinging on – by putting these, individually microscopic, things into laminated plastic folders. But, despite buying the plastic folders, I couldn't work out how to organise them.

*

On an April morning
seen outside-in
the mediocrity of the
recently gone – her
duffel coat, for one,
and the slung ledge
underneath the pushchair
shoved tight by a shoe
box, frondy fennel tops,

and the same cat we
stopped for, miaowing
tinnily beside the same
fancy an ice cream double-
sided Walls sign. The same
indefinite weather, lifting.

And that sickling down
bend forward from the hips
fiddling with the rain hood
rearranging something –
listening to the pattern of
breathing deepening:
why should time only
in taking things, in
handing down, make
what they were all along
flare to brilliance,
and the toddler sleeping.

4. London 2019/20

Last summer I started going back to the houses of my childhood. I could hardly explain why. Apparently, it's not an uncommon desire, in people of a certain age.

My daily commute takes me over Greenford and the southern tip of Northolt, where I was born. Literally over: the A40 is elevated on thin concrete pillars and underneath there's Greenford roundabout with the Harvester still on the corner.

For years I took the bus over this roundabout with no particular curiosity, only a calm, satisfied sense – having moved back from America, where time and space were always changing in concert, so new years brought new landscapes – that there was now a depth to my existence, because the present was bolstered by the past.

Then it changed. I had a sabbatical and more time. Now I found myself veering away from the flyover if I was in the car. I told myself that I was making short cuts of my own, having lost faith in Waze. In fact, the short cuts turned out to be anything but; the thick, clotted traffic would soon disperse and move loosely down the A40. But, by that point, I would be driving almost entirely at random and badly, close to tears, not indicating, around streets of interwar houses in Perivale or Greenford.

*

As I drove, I started wondering if this was *it*, the still centre of my life, the point, the marrow: me. Suddenly, I'd done all the things; all the life events had happened. And, without anything left to do, the things I'd already done disarranged themselves and became strung out and structureless. Now the only life event left was dying and, as my nan used to say, *those people that saw themselves shooting down the long white corridor, well, they were never dead, were they?*

Sometimes I parked, manoeuvring with difficulty, and walked around taking photos on my phone and listening to podcasts where Stephen Shore talked about snapshots. I spent a long time crouching down and worrying about the angles, not because I knew what angles I was trying to achieve, but because something was self-evidently wrong with most of the images: houses bulged aggressively in wedges towards the camera, and pavements sheered confusingly away. Giving up on perspective, I focused on pops of colour: a bright green garage door, the fleur-de-lys on garden railings dipped in gold and, round the porch, geranium brocades, straggly and tall.

The possibility of the shot dissolved if anyone entered the frame. And I could never find my car. Nonetheless, there was a glazed-over, confused pleasure in the driving, like waking up on a sunny morning late and realising that it's a Saturday and dozing until the room is very bright and then going down into the kitchen and picking with a fork at cold chicken casserole. The silky layer of congealed fat. Then coffee.

*

I wanted all of it again to do again.
A grown-up spoon. A thumbnail
puncturing a daisy stem,

spare floppy disks, that silver
paper from fresh cigarettes.
And a blue-grey flimsy night in June,
a lid that won't quite fit the day,
the boxwood yellowing in strips.

So, last summer, next, a profligate
excess of summertime to come,
and walking home at tip of dawn,
as a yellow awning is poled down
and the future is as cleft
and fuzzily unripe as peaches
swung inside a paper prism,
saved up to look forward to,
but also capable of blandness.
A future sensitive to error.

　　*

I also wanted all of it again
to piss away . . .
self-smartingly . . . the way
my toddler jutted out his chin
and looked away as tears
splat-mattified the pale
pressed Swanage sand around
his jelly shoes, his toes
a half size hidden from the end.

Because if cones are not
a thing that can *in ultimam*
be trusted in – all locked-down
spring we'd weighed up waffle cones
what green the mint in mint choc chip

should be – the fondant white
in After Eights, spruce green or lime? –
what was there but the *via
negativa*, the renounced?
What good were joyless *cups* stuffed
messily by hands in latex gloves
with raspberry ripple, each stripe
bunchy and refrozen, crystalline?

*

A single image kept coming to mind, perhaps it began in a dream. When it was snowing and the bars in Harvard Square closed early, we used, sometimes, to creep into the back room of a dilapidated undergraduate drinking club to drink more beer and play pool. There must have been music, but I don't remember what it was. This was 2005 or so. Maybe the Scissor Sisters.

None of it mattered, only the image of a sophomore girl in a backless cocktail dress – against the instinct of the season – dancing with a canister of whipped cream held in her hand, first to sync to, a kind of microphone, and then – as she got down lower and lower to the ground – fired inside her open mouth, aimed at her tonsils. There was cream everywhere, tinged pink by her lipstick. It looked for a moment like a disaster in a barber's shop and then her tongue flicked out quickly and licked everything up.

Was this such an interesting thing to do, or was I so easily disturbed in my complacency? Why remember it? Everyone then was very weight-conscious; it was the era of size 0. In Greenwich Village, the Olsen twins wandered around in complicated layers of embroidered toile and mohair, holding coffee cups like chalices. One of them – it was of course hard to say which – wore blue surgical gloves.

As the girl danced, two budding wings of fat slapped out of the back of her strappy cocktail dress. And the way she moved was contemptuous, somehow, as well as sinuous. I admired everything about her. But why? Was it the fuck-you air of unretreating rebellion, so different from my own self-conscious footling around, one step forward one step back?

*

The only intermission from driving was when I went to the supermarket. In the 1980s the building was new. Now it was dishevelled and complicated. But it didn't look just old, harmoniously old – the way a thatched cottage sprouts with grass and looks as if it might soon subside into the soil. It looked failed. There remained, despite its age, an insolent attitudinising futurism about the design – brutalism without the concrete.

I did my shopping hurriedly and then sat in the cafe until the street market outside closed and the carpark was dark, and children started appearing in the aisles in their uniform.

*

Drinking refilled cup
(free refills) after cup of
milkless heavily frothed-up
hot chocolate, sweetly taupe,
the bubbles webbed or latticed,
stiffly rendered by the gelatin,
I watched a man retract his pen,
the crossword done, replump
his thick felt navy hat, and then,
when friends sat down, say something
that I couldn't hear; his voice,

though – chewy, smoky, blackly
confidential, county Cork pre-war –
was so much like my father's
father thirty years ago,
his oxygen pulled out,
his cuffs rolled up, the swede diced
thickly in the wide flat-bottomed
dish, my father scurrying,
that my spine went flat against
the moulded plastic of the booth,
retracting.

The lino had a pattern,
it was common then,
of squares that spiralled on themselves
self-edified, but somehow
also hooked on to the next,
proud crests that never broke
and which I thought of, grandly,
as being *Roman*. Eventually,
the dustpan minus brush
was always needed, someone's
glass or mug being trashed
across the pattern, smithereens.

*

An upcycled bookcase in setting plaster pink. A memoir trans-
lated from Iranian on an E Ink reader not made by Amazon.

High hoppy beer in the fridge from local microbreweries: the
bottles unwaisted and stout, low ABV.

New ways of using up the aggressively perpetual turnips in farm
boxes, the sponge-like roots diced fine or blanched.

Coenzymated vitamin supplements. The pleasure of forwarding online petitions. Unwaxed lemons whole inside boiled puddings.

Instagram photos of slim books with white covers, skewed, beside worn Birkenstocks.

It could all go fuck itself.

*

The places that I wanted to revisit included Perivale public library, Hanger Lane Tube station, beside the Hanger Lane Gyratory System, the two storeys of offices on Acton High Street above the shops, the Cuckoo Estate in Hanwell, with its wide grassy verges and cul-de-sacs, and the post-war Catholic churches of the outer suburbs.

Eventually, I hoped to look with a beneficent eye at the stained glass in Our Lady of the Visitation in Greenford, and to sit, just sit, in the wooden pews of Saint John Fisher, listening to rush hour clog the A40, lapping the smell of incense, diesel and parquet polished with balsam.

To begin with, I wanted to overcome an instinctive revulsion from eroded or encrusted concrete, windows made from repeated grid shapes, and modern stained glass.

The things that I instinctively saw as ugly I wanted to see also, under another aspect, as beautiful.

*

The first inkling of success came with a shade of brown.

Several years ago, the Australian government asked Pantone to discover the most universally disliked colour. They wanted to discourage smoking by aversion, and planned to splash the most hated colour, whatever it should be, across cigarette packets. White boxes would be left for the risk warnings, and photos of oxygen masks and volcanic, gangrenous toes. The colour they came up with even has an unpleasant name: opaque couché. It has been described as filth, death, and meconium. It's a very brown olive green, a brown so lightly leavened by green that the overall effect is of a violent bout of diarrhoea occasionally diversified by up-chucked bile.

I knew the colour looked familiar but couldn't identify anything that really was that colour. I only made the connection late in the afternoon, waiting outside the hospital, on a dusty end-of-August day. I was waiting for someone to come out and looking in the rear-view mirror. Eventually I noticed my eyes.

*

After this, the new aspect began unassertively to dawn. A few weeks later we went to buy school uniform at a shop off the Fulham Road. You were meant to have an appointment. As a mother, I never knew these things. I saw my hopelessness in the way the manager snapped her tape measure shut, so the little silver tab retracted to her waist. If we wanted to come back at 3 . . .

The shop was just south of Charing Cross Hospital, on a narrow and congested side street that must, you assumed, have seen better days. It was an unforgiving area of London now.

We went and ate a pepperoni pizza at a cafe round the corner. It looked out onto the shuttered-up front of The Southern Belle ('Best Mangal') and a betting shop, which was doing a brisk trade. A pigeon with only two very long toes left was eating the end of a cream cheese bagel. Cars spritzed the pavement, the rain went on and off, a mother kept pulling a muslin cloth over a pram, and, when I tried to cut the pizza, the knife pulled at the thin dough rather than slicing through it. There was something dermatological about the dough's flaccidity.

The sun fell suddenly across the street, through the railings and plane trees outside the hospital, across the notched sculpture of a spine, and across the main entrance and terraces of windows. And, as I looked up, I saw how clear and kind the widely spaced plain font was: Charing Cross Hospital. Duck egg blue. Before, the terraces of windows had looked fussy but, with the sun still falling, I began to see the latticed rows not from the outside but internally, as the frame for an individual room.

And I imagined lying in a starched white bed for a week, surrounded by flowers, eating bowls of tinned peaches and condensed milk and watching day-time quiz shows on the ward's small TV. Or lying in a cot in the communal nursery making out a brightness when the winter sun came through the windows. I wanted the security of it: my bed made, tea from an urn, today's paper, quiet words with the woman in the next bed, the nurse's regular rounds. And the peace: the winter light falling through the windows, my tablets in a frilly paper cup, some sparrows. I wanted to lie on the ward smoking, looking at the sparrows, sometimes napping, and I wanted it cradle to grave.

*

If I drove through Greenford and South Harrow and stopped to let every pedestrian across,

and learned how frequently parades of shops occurred in interwar estates, what *precincts* meant.

If I could check the time on my Sekonda watch, drink
sparkling Moussec

and think about careers in the police,

or *keep the Common Market talking* as a French-speaking
telephonist,

wear raglan sleeves and Ken Hague overalls in nylon.

If I could get a Finnish massage at the Shangri-la.

And take a confidential £2 test to see: mother-to-be
or not-to-be?

If I could be remade in my own image of adulthood.

I bought bags of flying saucers and ate them in secret after
the children were in bed.

Only my adult tongue was too strong and instead of gently
excavating the pastel-coloured rice-paper for sherbet grains
it tended to puncture it.

What I wanted was a glimpse of something to believe in that
was communal

And still to come.

*

In October 1965, the leader of Kensington Council's Housing
Committee invited a young architect, Clifford Wearden, to pre-
sent plans for developing 23 acres in the north of the Borough

around Lancaster Road. He suggested building one 20-plus-storey tower block, with a parking space for each flat in the basement, and a number of three and four storey blocks ('to avoid the use of lifts') consisting of flats or maisonettes as required. There would also be a sorting office, four pubs, four doctors, two dentists, a nursery for fifty children, two halls for indoor games, and commercial premises available for letting.

After he had finished his presentation, questions were taken from the floor.

Q: How are mothers with prams and invalids going to get from level to level?
A: It is proposed to have ramps, which are essential also for the delivery of milk and parcels.

Q: A tragic characteristic of North Kensington is the indifference of the council to fire precautions. What of the people in these blocks when they catch fire? Will there be a new fire station?
A: A fire station has not been requested. It is not for us to say. The GLC is going to build a new station in Ladbroke Grove.

Q: What density is proposed for the new area, and what is the existing density?
A: We don't know how to work the proposed density out. We would like to have the same number of people as live there already, because we will have introduced many more amenities.

He noted that there was a mandatory requirement of 1008 parking spaces for the housing units, and that this would increase in the future.

*

'I want to listen to the tape of Mummy, I don't want *songs*.'

Our car was so old that it had a cassette player and I'd stuffed three tapes I found in my parents' garage into the glove box. In the recordings I was eight, maybe ten, and my voice was breathy and light. A friend and I were pretending to make a radio programme. In the first, I asked Katie to explain what people ate in China. In the second, she asked me questions about learning the double bass. I recommended a particular type of rosin, and discussed when I would be old enough to move to a three-quarter-size instrument.

The weirdest thing was that we had what could only be described as *historical* intonation. Up and down, up and down, riding the scale, barely a pause until the hard right edge of the nuclear stress.

We sounded like Princess Margaret.

*

There was a day when, suddenly
5′2″, some cello competence
achieved (though not much
'musicality'), they let you
try the double bass, a half-sized
one you borrowed from the
third-floor music room
and lugged downstairs,
sweat cornicing along the
dogtooth summer dress
(the front with tucks in now,
a bust dart for the breasts
you'd wait another decade
to arrive before going braless).

Unzipped at home, the ridgy
high-gloss nylon – like an
army bag, but padded –
spat a magpie hoard
of metal squares, some ripped,
some dangling stringy
colourless shed skins
across the oatmeal rug.
But when you bent to pick
them up your mother's
urgent minor third *Jo-*
ohn – as sad but naggingly
insistent as *hey Jude* –
flew up the stairs
Jo-ohn
(years later, when the music
teacher left his wife,
those wrappers
how he spent his lunch-times
doesn't bear much . . .)
and then, the misting on the wood
sponged clean, the wooden
stool spun up to height,
the bow hairs greasy with
that Olbas oil near-colourless
thick wax spelled *rosin*
everything felt braced and ached,
mutely too tight, the heavy
scoliosis-stricken bow just
smacking at the A string's
braided metal cable with a
scuffing sound like masonry
being hammered into chips
or wrecked by ball.

Jo-ohn you try it out
and realise that it's anyway
exactly how you call your
sons and husband down,
slipping the just-done peas
from sieve to bowl.

5.   Northolt, July 2020

Towards the end of the heatwave, I drove to Oldfield Circus in Northolt, where my life had begun, and sat on a bench in the middle of the roundabout. The photo was so easy to see that I didn't even need to take it.

It was the day after my father's 70th birthday, the first decade he hadn't seen, and I cried for all of it: the front door with its cloudy bobbled glass, the strung-up gooseberries at the back of the garden, even the smell of the silver paper in the cigarette packets that I tried, sanctimoniously, to hide from him. After he'd given up, he chewed polos instead as he drove to work, listening to cassettes on positive thinking. I even cried for that, the brittle crunch of sugar on dental enamel.

*

The redness of the letterbox,
The Crawford butchers sign,
The cursive *OPEN*.
How we bought pears.
My father, 70 today,
his first whole decade missed,
the napkins (*please stop smoking!*)
that I coloured in felt tip
and slotted under every
bevelled ashtray in the house,
my mother's womb biopsied,

hacked about and binned,
that bit of home, like all homes lost,
the toddler treading on a crab
and jumping on white sand
giddy in my arms, shell-strewing,
how mired I was in time,
still drowsing in my pushchair
lolling in the sun's old net
beneath the tree scrunched
up with blossom fists,
how we bought pears, beside
the door still waiting for
the gate to click, how mired
I was in time there was no
record of or memory
otherwise now anywhere.

*

Then I bought a Tango at the newsagent, and walked very slowly past the pub, round the corner, onto the street where I was born. The pavement couldn't have been expanded – it was always very wide – but now it had been refaced with a smooth yellow stone. Hydrangeas brimmed over the remaining walls and bougainvillea still grew round the front door, where I used to stand waiting for my father to come home from work. A receding line of traffic cones, some fallen over, repeated the colour pattern on the left-hand side of the photo.

'Lived round here long?' I asked, unable to think of anything better. It was a cold, sharp March morning and my sinuses hurt. In the gutter a pigeon was exploring a long strip of orange peel, flattened to a map.

The woman outside number 39, on the other side of the road, was doing something complicated with two bins. I made a flaccid gesture of offering to help – knowing that the full-hearted version of the gesture would now seem like a threat.

*

When the gardener's gone and the roses crisp up like a pinched pair of teabags stuck to a spoon,

And the once unexceptional post-war consensus is a clearly quixotic mid-century whim,

When, Europe now over, you trawl around Lidl, and reach for a Spanish-style platter of ham,

But the two-metre gap is too long for your arms, so you panic, the mask riding into your teeth like a thong.

Sorry.

Then the time left to come and the time that has gone will be placed in the pans of the scale and find balance.

Sorry.

*

'Round here? Oh yes it's changed, definitely changed.'
　　'My mum's died now. I'm not from round here. I'm just clearing out some of her things.
　　'But yes, these last few years. You get a very different sort of people. Always moving on, can't be bothered to keep the place up. See.'

I explained that I'd lived in the house opposite as a child and was trying to remember it. 'But that was twenty years ago,' I said, unlocking the door of the car. 'Actually, thirty.' Rather pointlessly, I then observed, 'all of the houses used to have front gardens'.

On my noticeboard at home there was a photo where I was learning to walk, taken by my father. I was pushing a small red truck across the pavement onto a wide tarmac verge. Behind, you could see the neighbours' wall and ours, which was missing its small decorative ball (a finial?). Now there were hardly any walls left. The laburnum tree in the front garden had also gone. Once I'd put some of the dry grey berries up my nose, excited first by the sharp smell, and then by how many would slip in. I lined them up like peas. An hour later – parental panic about poisoning – the eyewatering sensation, almost a rush, of cold metal tweezers pinching them out, one by one.

As I got back into the car, I realised that it wasn't thirty years ago. The street was built on wooded land in 1937, ten years after the Tube station at Northolt Park was opened. And I was born in 1979. So it was forty years and a whole half of the house's lifetime ago. 'You take care', she said suddenly, lifting a hand stiffly. The salute was framed by the clean curtainless window behind her.

I pulled slowly away, mashing through the gears. At the top of the street, near a wire-fenced lane that ran through scrubland, a girl of three or four was standing with her mother in the doorway of a tall, recently built house. They were both wearing violet dressing gowns. No one seemed to be coming or going, they weren't waving goodbye, they weren't exuberantly expecting. They were just standing with calm impassive faces as if they would be standing there forever.

*

The superimposition
of the figure on the ground
appearing only later,
after . . .

At first the almost colourless
fine hair cut in a helmet
(Caramac) and brick and grouting
and the stained glass of the lemon
chiffon door merged and recurred,
as did the St George's cross of
sock and T-bar strap (bright red),
repeated on the sewn-on
pocket of the smock –
and this despite the motion blur,
the offset of the shutter speed
and child's deliberate steps,
the galaxies of whitewash
(painters in?) and next door's
twitchy pleated nets . . .

It was all bland, harmonious,
and given to us:
a ravishing for-nothingness.

HAPPY BIRTHDAY

. . . aperitque futura

1.

The first half having been
given up to space, I decided
to devote my remaining
life to time, this thing we live
in fishily or on like moss
or the spores of a stubborn
candida strain only to be
gored or gaffed, roots
fossicked out by rake or have
our membranes made so permeable
by azole drugs the contents
of the cell flood everywhere.

The bubble gun I'd bought
on Amazon had come
so, time's novitiate, flushed,
I stood outside the door
in velour slippers with a plastic
wedge, from M&S, the toes
gone through, and practised
pulsing softly on the trigger,
pushing dribbly hopeless sac
shapes out, dead embryos
that managed, all the same,
to right themselves to spheres,
and bob as bubbles do, the colour
of a rainbow minced or diced
into the laurel bush or else
just brim the fatal fence, most

out of reach of the toddler
capering side to side to keep
his balance on the grass, one
snotty index finger poised
in threat of threat until,
five seconds in, they self-unskinned
and lost their radiance,
re-rendered air.

This would have been in that
sad hobbled stretch of week
between a Sunday Christmas
and new year, my friends all
40+, harassed by infants, joylessly
still slugging back the red,
the detox books not downloaded
to app but only browsed by phone
in bed, the year stuck self-
indulgently at its nadir,
dawn wet and recusant.

It wasn't till my birthday,
January 3rd, when schools went back,
search engines saw a volume
spike for 'custody' and gifs of
sullen cats with emery boards
explained the dead-eyed un-
sheathed fear produced by credit
card repayment plans and pissing
on ketosis sticks that the month
could manifest the rawness
of new year: poverty then,
and mock exams; now, enzyme
supplements, and softening

the 11s, scooped one layer
deeper by all that red wine,
by summer's oxidative damage.

2.

The dry trees lolled in drunken
groups outside front gates,
waiting for the council van
to come. Today, which was
my birthday, they were taken
off, undressed, along with
twenty near-identical
reception Christmas cards:
the cotton-wool-ball snowmen
shaggy now, and noseless.
And even Neutradol could
not disguise the rancidness
of nappies from the 24th,
threaded by the bin in strings,
an evenness about the links
like sausages or those stiff
poodles men with toupees
used to fashion from balloons.

My son propped on one hip,
front door ajar, both shivering
in the not yet dawn, the heating
just about to crackle on,
raised up his palm in silent
salutation at the work being done.
One man, his shoulders dewy

with reflective strips, waved
back and called him by his name
– the weekly ceremony –
until he bristled in my arms
with happiness, legs stiffening.

His dragon trouser legs,
green tessellating scales,
were halfway to the knee, so
soon they'd be bagged up or binned.
The scene of decathexis:
his bedroom floor, the mini
palm tree on the balcony
opposite wind-combed, sparse;
sun spotlighting my calves
which had the shiny wide-pored
look my mother's had, once,
on a short brown beach in France,
her dirndl skirt hoiked up, frites
frying at the wooden shack
as I span pebbles sulkily
over the unmoving water
out to the island, the dinghy
where my father lay in state,
napping.

3.

Downstairs I mixed some Movicol
into warm juice and saw a
squirrel run across the grass,
freeze skinny as a meerkat

on the mostly mud I'd tried
to reseed twice last summer.
(After moss killer, waiting,
something ferrous, the shady
lawn seed recommended by
a friend eventually produced,
as if by staple gun, a few sparse
fiercely emerald reeds, which died.)

Both boys had scrambled over
look! and when they turned away
behind the mouth and nose
breath diamonds, fading now,
the squirrel was spray-digging,
pelleting again, even though
he must have polished off his nuts
by Halloween. We'd seen him,
bushier then, a baby really,
slyly going back and back,
as we did on school coach trips
to the battlefields of Ypres
ripping through the Monster Munch
long before the sickening ferry
with its waffle smell and slot
machines, the textbook poppy
fields we'd seen on *Blackadder*,
in reality redder.

I suppose the squirrel didn't know
the days would stick like curtains
catching on the outer edge
of metal track, the yellow
fleur-de-lys a half-inch less
wide open every morning.

I knew that I could probe it,
Hey Siri, do squirrels tend to
survive their first winter
in urban or semi-urban
environments? but the fact
that I was always ladling
porridge as he dug, donating
raisins, doing calligraphy
with smooth or crunchy
peanut butter – there was
that whole jack-o'-lantern
month, involving apricots,
when it rained – only added
to my sense of having been
complicit in his losses:
the bad grass, the Amazon
deliveries that kept coming
in white Toyota vans, the
part-thawed corn cobettes
siloed in their own brown bag,
spongy with a mortuary
softness that repelled me.
He'd seen all that.

The boys had gone upstairs
– a long withdrawing roar of
Avalanche!, the scuff of
falling cushions – so I grabbed
a handful of cashews and stood,
unseen outside the window,
scattering them contritely on
the mud, around the reeds
now colourless, and the small
quill of his wavering tail.

4.

So, yes, it was New Year and
then my birthday yet again
and, as my son reminded me,
this year it was a prime.
Last year had been the big 4-
0, so lots of cards whose faux
light-hearted 'you'll be needing
glasses' riffs – in fact, I'd
had them from being 6 –
and 'if I'd got a funny card
you'd piss yourself, at your age'
led to a grim, inexorable
nunc est bibendum theme:
something about be-ginning.

It was the thirteenth prime,
I looked it up. Another
six and I'd be 71, then on
the swift downhill but splashily
prime-punctuated, it turned out,
grave run. Because, however,
I was born in 1979,
another prime, and at its start,
on a day when frogmen
crawled the ponds on Hampstead
Heath for boys who'd fallen
through the popping ice,
a woman paralysed by polio
was burnt to death with both her
infant daughters in the house,
and a pig that had been stabbed
with ricin on a tiny pin

died just as the Bulgarian
spy had done, and with the same
derangements of blood chemistry,
the chance of both my own age
and the year's being free
of all divisors was minute –
two days at 47, 59,
73 . . .

5.

What else: the sum of two
adjacent squares, the dialling code
for Switzerland and Mozart's
final symphony in C
the sublime Jupiter . . .
Also, on a blustery day
in Oxford in the fifties,
early May, the number
worn askew, slung under-rib
by Roger Bannister, as lifting
up his chin he let his mind
draw just outside his body
and convulsed, pale as a
pierrot on someone in a
many-lapelled mac and trilby.
The time, said the announcer,
shouting in the wind, was three . . .
Three . . .

In Mexico the number's still
taboo, you bypass it entirely

straight to 42. And in Japan,
where everyone's born one,
it's an unlucky year for men.
Oppenheimer found himself
the father of the atom bomb;
'So death doth touch the resurrection,'
he quoted from John Donne.
If anyone had bloody hands
it was the president, said Truman.

The search bar asked: a 7 in shoes,
too young to cash your pension in,
too old for IVF own eggs,
have one last baby as a man.
The famous people who had died
included Alan Turing,
whose macabre poisoning
by cyanide-laced apple
was memorialised on various
products that I owned
(he liked the Disney film),
and Austen, possibly from
arsenic (she said her face
went black and white).
Even Shakespeare feared his powers
were spent, his poems all done,
and nothing coming out in print,
not even an old play, revised.
Hamnet was a decade dead.
He was afraid of treason,
eclipses of the moon and sun,
court machinations, blindness.
He wrote his worst play, *Timon*.
And then he wrote:

Nothing will come of nothing.
Speak again.
He wrote *tomorrow and tomorrow*
and tomorrow.

6.

Sometimes I liked being dizzied
to my knees like this by surplus
screen shit, random querying:
NO-REPLY Appt reminder
Hope you have a lovely day
the almost blithe transcendent
brain dysfunction of the total
lack of focusing, the shimmer
sideways I could feel my right
eye blur to as I stood,
so puzzled, worrying at the book
I'd butchered in the stacks
by accident . . .

The osteoporotic spine
all particles, frayed ribbon,
skin stubs, moving in the
light that, falling from the west
(where home was, where my son
would wait soon in the going-
home room with his coat on)
was weirdly dark and definite,
like when your fork pulls at
the slouchy bag of a pre-made
swirled in vinegar corn-fed

poached egg, and the ochre yolk
is slashed across the English
muffin, cooling hollandaise,
and fine sac, couldn't quite
say scrotal, of the albumen.

About to shower, I couldn't see
much me-ness in the mirror
just the wry grin of my scar,
the second better than the first,
but still lopsided, run on
the diagonal. In China
health authorities alarm
as virus tally reaches 44
in capital of Hubei province
Wuhan, I could have read,
if I'd read every piece of news
that day. I didn't, of course.

7.

οἶσθα γὰρ εὖ περὶ τέρμαθ᾽
ἑλισσέμεν. We read Homer
once, in a small attic room
with a map of the world
known to the Greeks tacked
over the white board, *orbis
Herodoti*, neat as a kidney,
and shaded boiled shrimp
(British India pink):

termat': the plural of terma
the boundary or goal that
horses turn round in a race.

elissemen: turn
inf act + poetic
to turn at the doublingpost,
wheel round the horses.

'Mark then the goal,' wrote Pope,
'. . . of some once-stately oak
the last remains, or hardy fir,
unperished with the rains . . .
(some tomb perhaps of old . . .)'
The key bit though, the 'nussa'
he left out: it meant the
turning or exact midpoint,
as of a race or life,
in Latin it was *meta*.

A Freudian slip?
He'd just turned 30
and hated birthdays.
By 35, encompassed by
the hourly expectation
of her death, 'poor Mother
seems but upon the whole
to wait for the next cold Day
to throw her into a Diarrhoea
that must, if it return, carry her off.'
And then, 'Is that a birthday?
'tis alas! too clear, 'tis but
the funeral of the former year.'

8.

I googled menopause:
The Slow Moon Climbs
The Panic Years and then,
on Google Books, I read about
the box-like reproductive
pattern shown by barbary
macaques and lions, and how this
differed from the weirdly long
post-reproductive life spans
women have – by this point, I
was sitting on the bed, naked,
trying to pinch the page into
full screen – we were frontloaders,
it explained, skewed left,
weaning our helpless
altricial offspring sooner
than baboons to pack more in
before, around the age of 41
(consistent as the median age
for final birth across a
wide range of societies
dispersed in time and place)
sterility set in . . .

A little wedge of time
I'd spent on nothing much,
New Year after New Year
finding me playing pinball
or sitting, high, in a Mission
dive bar with naugahyde
booths beneath a lit-up
triptych of our Lady Guadalupe

listening to the gasping poof –
a succulent sound – of someone
in suspenders and a trilby
thrashing a dog piñata
till it split and candy corn
and drumsticks tumbled down,
the tamale lady picking up
stray wrappers from her cart
as she went round.

The message seemed to be
that all the things I'd always been
surprised to have been given,
to do with sex, were being removed,
or had been while I slept, or
something, and the body that
I got to go on living in
would be a curio, a thing that,
having lost its use value,
is taken from the mantelpiece
to polish, pass around, almost
unchanged, breasts unretreating,
a waist left to be dressed,
forms mapped too easily to their
once-function, lost now. I felt
the same creep of disgust
when I saw a peacock lugging
round his broken tail,
stray feathers at odd angles,
the central bone hung down,
like the rattan on an eBay chair
sold for upcycling only and
tap, tap-tapping the ground.

9.

It would be months before
I lay unblinking on the bed
and worked the chalk two
paracetamol had left across
my gums with lemon squash,
a pint, while searching, finally
for what was happening:
pleurisy, rib pain, cut glass
opacities, I thumbed, and read
the feeds of people in Berlin
disputing quarantine R0
pathogen the Princess Diamond
why cocoons are never safe,
then watched a video of snow
massing right to left across
the scientist's window in Pankow
until it was the only medium
and all the rosy hologrammed
interior – his shaggy head
the MacBook Pro – had been
replaced by monochrome:
the avenue he lived on with
its scrub of park and single
taxi turning right, the Moomin-
softened lines of parked-up cars
which, like the tramlines
and the avenue of linden trees,
reached to the grey horizon's
grainy limit.

10

Pankow: I went there once,
heard jazz, drank amaretto sours –
the era of Geheimclubs,
pre-internet. A Nil light fog.
Someone had brought a cat . . .
One night I went back with
the only bona fide hot man
I had ever fucked, we sat
beside his stone-fired oven,
smoked up, laughed manically,
ate sushi; once we visited
a huge East German statue
of a book, made out of iron,
his fingers fiddling with
my gingham dress's straps,
then bunching up the skirts
to slide inside them, lie there.
Afterwards I had an urge
to lay my index finger
down his nose and feel straight bone,
also my speech, so halting
normally, surprised me in its
glibly dirty fluency, e.g.
sitting, facing the oven's
dying orange rectangle,
riding him only slightly, widely,
whole metaphoric sets replaced
my usual simple clutch of low
percussive English sounds.

Now, though, on my birthday,
a twenty-year sagged span,

what I remembered wasn't that –
lost German words, old
recklessness, even his name –
but the chesty froth *do doo
be do* of the woman in the jazz
club singing scat, which seemed,
with forty years to go, the chord
progression tediously fixed,
the apter metaphor, the sound
pushed at the room and carried,
higher than the cigarette smoke,
floating.

11.

Is there anything you want?
the message ran midscreen
a banner from my mum.
A chocolate smartie cake?
my son said, with the confidence
of someone who had made
(OK, dictated furiously)
a list of every birthday cake
he hoped for all the way
from 5, next month, to 32
– beginning with a fondant-
fanged *T. rex* and ending via
a white-piped fox with Marshall.

I'd never even known which
dog was which in Paw Patrol,
made *chocolate gingermen,*

or sat, while he still cared,
beside him in the park watching
the nesting moorhens.

Later, after serous cells were found,
and everything was taken out,
sewn up, the cervix gone,
like a heelless sock or any
lazily ruched thing, abhorring
vacuum, it was this, the list –
his I suppose untrammelled in
us all numeric innocence,
each birthday like the last,
bland adding on – that she
broke down at.

Already June. Outside,
the daisies turned their faces up,
shockingly bright – plain
as the clock I'd started on
at school, and then left handless
after splitting four saws zing!
on Perspex. Her neighbour
prowling with his watering can
would pass and gently part them.
He'd studied botany, she said,
served in Suez. We'd brought him
16 of the strawberry shakes
(the proteins hydrolysed,
plus riboflavin, carotene)
she'd been sent home with and,
as point of pride, not stomached.

During lockdown he'd lost weight,
his airtex scalloped at the waist,
and when he smiled his nose
moved with his upper lip,
a bobby-pinned French plait.
It's a rite of passage here,
we've all had cancer.
I followed him upstairs
and put the pink Nutricia shakes
in a tidy skittle shape
on the high-gloss parquet:
almost immaculate,
just one left over.

12.

'What does a woman want?'
The great unanswered question,
Freud said, in a letter to
the heiress Marie Bonaparte –
but he'd only had 30 years'
research; I'd now had 40.

How infantile, un-Zen,
the thing I wanted was
I couldn't help but know –
surprised though, all the same,
in this indifferent mizzly
blur of cloud and rain outside,
the radiator panging
for omeprazole, the birds
disorganised on gables,
by something in the solar

plexus, a swift upward cut
like heartbreak, diminishing . . .
(and therefore worse, the loss
of love being magnified by
loss of feeling for its squalled
magnificence).

I wanted all of it again
to do again, a thought that,
9 a.m. a Tuesday, Lego everywhere,
was filleting – by this point
I'd stuck Peppa on – my mouth
sour with the grit of living
like this, petrified in time,
without the lull of acquiescent
stillness even; no, more driven
on, like us in that packed car
oh years ago on the M1
southbound from Sheffield
after Christmas, presents stuffing
up the boot and trapped between
a lorry and a horsebox,
moving at the constant speed
the traffic had attained, two
chevrons separated, always,
as the radio found Capital.

Our car, a yellow Renault,
was by modern standards huge
but bashfully designed
as if the single grille
and boxy bonnet might
miraculously pipe the crude
back through the shattered

layers of rock into the under-
seabed sealed-off pockets
that we'd learned, in geography,
it poured from, gouting.

13.

In fact, this day, this nothing
happening still centre
bobbing buoy, where no
momentum for a second sways,
might be, as it was for
my grandmother who died
at almost 82 in perfect health
already past halfway –
the 30 seconds after noon
that pedants about time
notch up as late, but silently,
the minute hand still cleaving
nervously to 12, no thin white
wedge of clockface visible,
or the line a child draws out
in black felt tip, traced almost
perfectly.

I wanted all of it again to do again
and this time pay attention
to the way things showed,
the ends lodged immanently
from the start. The way a
fuzzy very small green bud, just
saved from last week's frost

gives some suggestion of its
way of going out sun-shrivelled,
colourless.

14.

The first half having been
given up to space, I decided
to devote my remaining
life to time, this thing we
neither chuff from the exhaust
so, at each juncture, being now
somewhere new, it's guzzled up,
choking particulate,
nor currents left in brain cells that
can be, in certain kinds of snow,
rum-drunkenness, or when
the stovetop coffee whistles
higher in a rented gîte, re-cued.

The metaphors were wrong.
It wasn't, after all, the sea,
compacted soil, damp folds
of sweaty skin – a medium
to live in, opportunely,
till the bitten hook the scratchy
rake the shocking intimation
of the sun the gaping cell:
then there would have to be,
as well as time, some other
time-type thing to choose instead.
And there was none.

No, not so purposive,
more kinked and eddying,
a thing to bob or stall in,
just as once, in vaporous early
morning heat in Guerneville,
after goat cheese avocado toast,
we watched the rails of fog
being lifted from the river,
then hired inflatables and tubed
from Steelhead all the way to
Sunset Beach in wavering lines
of bright pink rubber rings.
My own ring as the day went on
got tangled in the reeds, bank-
gravelled, so I had to scrabble
with my toes, push off against
fine shingle at each bend,
joined sometimes on the bank
or for a ragged oscillating drift
by someone else: a friend,
the boy whose nose I blazed
with suncream like a horse.

Downstream, the cooler with
the high-hopped session ales,
the ice and cherry popsicles,
kept sailing in its unicorn
canoe a little pompously
right down the river's centre
where the water braided
faster to the dark Pacific.
We found it on a sandbar
where a man was grilling fruit,
the cooler tipped and beached,

the ice a handful of soft shapes.
I tried to grab your dinghy back
he said – and then broke off,
his open palm extended
vaguely, speckled with cilantro,
not to the next steep wooded
crook, or eyot where the river
split in two, but with a loose
indefiniteness, a more
generally downriver sign –
towards the estuary where
smolt adapt to saltwater,
go silvery and shoal
and later will return
full-grown to spawn.

15.

I'd love a chocolate cake,
I wrote, *and they would too,*
maybe some buttons on?
And then I started calling
boy-oys that minor third again
it's time to do your teeth
we're going out. A far-off
galloping downstairs and
as I waited, filling up the bowl,
a tallow-coloured moth,
square space-age wings,
perched on the white enamel rim.

Buy cedarwood, my mother said,
mothballs are banned.
But I'd done nothing more
than trying to recollect the smell.
What was it?
Naphthalene.
Adult, sharp, a bit like bleach
but sweatier, more volatile,
almost exciting in its
finnicky acknowledgment
of the way last winter's coat
sits quietly getting eaten out
on long June nights.
An old man's giddiness:
fetor hepaticus.

And then I watched as
almost flutterless it lay
companionably down
and spread its wings out flat
in benediction – I had knelt –
right on the pillow-shaped
meniscus of the water.
Why? No reason other than
each instant's disregard,
being self-contained,
for what might follow,
the flashiness of staring down
tomorrow.

Acknowledgements

'Tenants' is in memory of the seventy-two people, including an unborn baby, who lost their lives as a result of the fire in Grenfell Tower. The fire broke out on the fourth floor early on June 14, 2017.

The poem is based in part on material published during Phase 1 of the Grenfell Tower Inquiry.

I am indebted to my first readers for their generosity and patience. Thank you to my assiduous editors at Faber, Matthew Hollis, Lavinia Singer and Jane Feaver; to my agent, Sarah Chalfant, and to Alba Ziegler-Bailey and Luke Ingram at the Wylie agency; to Mitzi Angel at FSG; and to friends who read early versions of the poems, especially Declan Ryan and Clare Pollard.

A version of 'Tenants' was read aloud at the Coronet Theatre in 2019. Thank you to James Lever for his intelligent attention to the text of the poem and to all of those involved in the performance. The archivists at Kensington Central Library provided invaluable help in researching the history of Notting Dale and the Lancaster West Estate.

Parts of 'Happy Birthday' first appeared in *Liberties* magazine.

Epigraphs are from John Donne, 'To Sir Henry Wotton' ll. 55–57; William Wordsworth, *The Prelude* (1798–1799), ll. 1–6; Virgil, *Aeneid* VI.12. I am grateful to the T. S. Eliot Estate for permission to quote from *Four Quartets*.

My deepest thanks are to my husband, Ian Martin.

Printed in the USA
CPSIA information can be obtained
at www.ICGtesting.com
LVHW041610080724
784929LV00006B/144

9 780374 612863